The West Coast of Heaven

Other Books by Jack Moser

The Male Journey (2006)
We Have Forgotten How to Make Fire (2007)
The Murmur of a Gentle Breeze (2008)
If I Were Felled (2009)
Men in Therapy (2010)
You Can See Me From Here (2011)
I Love You to the Moon (2012)
The Wonder of it All (2013)
He Doesn't Have a Clue, Does He? (2014)
Who Cares? I Do. (2015)

The West Coast of Heaven

poems by

Jack Moser

Fithian Press, McKinleyville, California · 2016

Printed in the United States of America

Published by Fithian Press
A division of Daniel and Daniel, Publishers, Inc.
Post Office Box 2790
McKinleyville, CA 95519
www.danielpublishing.com

Distributed by SCB Distributors (800) 729-6423

LIBRARY OF CONGRESS CATALOGING-IN-PUBLICATION DATA
Names: Moser, Jack, [date] author.
Title: The west coast of heaven : poems / by Jack Moser.
Description: McKinleyville, California : Fithian Press, 2016.
Identifiers: LCCN 2016013971 | ISBN 9781564745880 (softcover : acid-free paper)
Classification: LCC PS3613.O77878 A6 2016 | DDC 811/.6—dc23
LC record available at https://lccn.loc.gov/2016013971

To the God of the West Coast of Ireland
who has given me fifteen years of
beauty and friendship beyond
what I could have ever imagined.

Thank you, Irish.

Contents

I. The West Coast of Heaven

II. Craziness

Part I

The West Coast of Heaven

The West Coast of Heaven

When an Irish person dies,
leaving their home on the West Coast
she goes straight up to heaven.
When she arrives it looks exactly
like the west coast of Ireland,
where she has just departed.
She asks God, "Is this really heaven?"
"Yes," responds God.
"This is it."

True, the rocks are softer
with celestial singing over loudspeakers.
Roads are made of marshmallow.
Fields can be walked upon
without sinking.
Food grows everywhere.
Yet, it looks identical to home.
Upon further inspection, however,
So much is missing.

There is no wind
No blackberry bushes
No loose chipping on roads
No rocky walls surrounding paths
No rain.
Give me a break!
I want my heaven on earth.
I want bluster
And bombast.
We shall have to change heaven
just a bit.

It is much like visiting a housing development
Where everything is bright and shiny.
God can turn the weather on and off.
No, thank you.
I want my west coast heaven,
Thank you very much!
Give me cow dung and torrential rain
and, God,
Don't mess around with my heaven.

How Can I Keep From Singing?

I am home again in Ireland.
People I love are here.
People I would gladly die for
Welcome me as if I were "someone."

In Ireland, I desire to be "no one."
I am surrounded by giants,
People who love you as if this were
the easiest activity in their lives,
"And, for them it is."

The Irish love you with this
steady diet of smiles, laughter, and embrace.
I am lifted above
to see life differently.
How can I keep from singing?
I cannot.

Irish Talent

It isn't the fact that Ireland
loves her arts.
It isn't the fact that what you see
and what you hear is beauty.
It is the fact that so many Irish
have so many artistic gifts,
So many sing and dance,
So many play more than one instrument.
Arts are the blood in their veins
They circulate into every artery
Bubbling forth in word and action.
Such a small country
fills the universe with joy.
"Fair play to you, Ireland."

The Stones Speak

Of all the natural beauty in Ireland,
the one most glorious item for me are the stones.
There are myriad walls
stretching everywhere in sight.
I never venture outside
without the stones speaking to me.

I see families in the bog
breaking large boulders into small stones.
I see them building walls
so to outline their property.
Each time I walk the roads
they speak to me.

They talk of the hard times
Of the famine and the wars
Of death and dying
Of the loving and the losing
Of all they saw
Of all they remember.

It is fascinating to me
that I can hear this
and see this.
Every day as I roam the paths
the stones speak.

I Learn From the Irish

I watch Irish people when I am here
Immediately, I notice, that
They are into the present moment
Whether it is comments about the weather
Or asking about family members
They are totally absorbed in the other.

Everyone seems to know each person they meet
Greetings are given as they stop
to pass on the news of the day.
Their eyes never waver from the other
They sound genuinely concerned.
I hear very little anger
I hear interest and humor.

They don't seem to be attempting
To score debate points in their repartee.
Easy, soft words
Comfortable laughter
Nothing to prove
Nothing to hide
Nothing but genuine friendship.

Gone Again

He is my Irish brother, Tony Whelan.
He is a "peacekeeper" in the Irish Army.
He left last week for a one-year tour
in Lebanon, close to Palestine.
I am heartbroken
I do not want him to be in harm's way
I pray for his safety.
Shekhinah will keep him
in the palm of her hand.*
Please bring him home.
There are so few
men of honor left in this world.
He is gone again.
Please carry him back
to us who love him.

**Shekhinah is the secret of possibility, the female God in Jewish mysticism.*

Plant Magic in the Bog

A mere leaf or fern, I think not.
Just inspect their domain.
Thousands of minute parts
working together to produce
a unique form and aura.

The bog has so much to teach us
about living and working together.
Chlorophyll, rain, sun, wind, birds, insects
all moving in unpredictable ways
to create wonder.

We brush these amazing creatures off
Not giving them the honor they deserve.
They give us life
So that we may flourish and
Embrace this wonder.

Essences are items we seem to miss
Yet everything belongs,
All of it
And us
If we so wish.

Time and Change

I have peered out of my large windows
onto the North Atlantic Ocean
for the past fifteen years.
Nothing in my view has changed.
As it was 12,000 years ago
It is now.
The wind emanating from God's throat
Thunders ashore,
The waves of all the world's oceans
caress the beaches and rocks,
Dolphins and seals pop up now and then
as they seem to do.
This land has changed me over the years.
My vision
My breath
My soul
coming together to celebrate
this majestic oneness.

Heather and Camille

Three years ago they appeared in this world.
I saw them when they were
just a few weeks old.
Now they have grown into healthy horses
easily resembling their mother.

I only experience their presence once per year
Yet as soon as I speak to them
Their ears shoot straight up
As they immediately amble over to me
where only a fence of stones stands between us.

Have you ever felt the head of a horse
resting on your heart?
It is a feeling kept alive in my mind.
That is my greeting.
They act as if I were a member of their family.

I ply them with apples and carrots
as they love on me,
This city boy is in "horse heaven"
Treated as a king in the West Ireland bog
by two Connemara ponies.

The Five Belgium Hikers

A knock on the front door
Five young female hikers
Just as sweet and innocent as you would hope
They would soon be asleep in the pasture with cows
But it was colder than they had anticipated
So they needed blankets
Plus I gave them my woolen pajamas
A knock on the front door
They used the bathroom
A knock on the door
They cleaned their dishes
What a delight they were!
They told us that Belgium
Was known as "the country of peace"
I could see why
Thank you Belgium
for rearing such amazing women.

Blackberry Picking, Again

I roam the paths of Errislannan
Picking the food of man
And, as in past years,
The berries see me coming
Commencing their incessant chanting of
"Take me, take me, please, take me"
I never quite get over this outcry
"Eat me, eat me, please"
They seem to believe
That if you eat them and enjoy the eating
They can then return to earth
Again to be picked from a roadside bush
To be eaten again by the hungry
People of the planet.
What greater gift for a plant is there?

Modernizing Ireland

Last year the roads on the West Coast
Were no longer covered with "loose chippings."
No. They were hard tar.
I was really upset
I love "loose chippings."

This year, you won't believe this,
They have painted a white stripe
Down the middle of the road.
Now I am really upset.
What is the rural west coast coming to?

What next?
Turn signals?
I am indeed perplexed,
I like one-lane roads,
I like pulling off to let a car go by.
What are the Irish thinking?

I would like cow paths and dirt roads,
No white lines down the middle,
Thank you very much.
No!
I shall put my foot down
But not on the surfaced roads.

Bugs

My friends the O'Connells
Found a rabbit in the road.
He was abandoned, so they
Brought him home to live with them.

"Bugs" has a cage in the backyard
Every day someone or something visits.
All the other animals seem to like him,
Though the cats seem to be licking their chops.

The first visitors were the local hares.
Bigger feet, bigger ears,
Yet they knew they were related.
The hares have tried to get Bugs out of his cage
To no avail.

The next visitors were the two cats,
Molly and Minnie.
They enjoy putting their noses on Bugs
But they also salivate as they touch him.

Every week the Connemara ponies arrive.
They push against the cage with their heads
But really don't seem to be close.
Following a few minutes they move on.

The best visitors are Mary and Joe.
They sit next to the cage,
They bring Bugs into the house
Where he sleeps on their laps.
There may be some hope for
These humans after all.

The Grafton Guest House Beanstalk

We are headed to Dublin
We got a really good deal on lodging
When we arrived at the Grafton
We realized why we had procured
A room so quickly
The Grafton Guest House is taller than Everest
After we had walked up hundreds of stairs
There was a man with grappling hooks
And rope for climbing
We climbed for thirty minutes
Before being placed aboard a small helo
which took us to the bottom of a beanstalk
Our room was atop the beanstalk
In our small room, there was no bathroom
Just a number of oxygen canisters and masks
Plus seat belts for the bed
If it was a windy night
The seatbelt sign was on at all times
When we couldn't get down in the morning
The Dublin Fire-Rescue helped us.

Tommy Ticket

You don't see many Garda
During the day in Clifden.
But once night falls,
It is an entirely different picture.

At midnight at the Garda station
The security gate slowly opens.
Out slips Tommy Ticket.
His job is to ticket all cars
That people left in town overnight.

He is difficult to spot
Since he is attired totally in black.
He seems to slither among vehicles
Heartlessly ticketing every auto,
Even ambulances, hearses, and fire trucks.

No one is immune from Tommy's wrath.
His job is "to ticket"
And ticket he does!
His wife's car?
You guessed it.

The Smoked Salmon Safe House

When I was working in Navy Intelligence
I spent three years with the CIA in Manila.
We were always looking for possible safe houses
To house fugitives or any agents or to hold meetings.
We needed a place not many people frequented,
A place where we could see someone coming
From a good distance away.

Today I was driving on the west coast of Ireland.
I was on narrow roads which were used by
Small cars, large cows, and sleek horses.
I was looking for a commercial outlet
Which had a great reputation for smoked salmon.
After a tortuous drive, I spied this building
Located at a long pier,
Not many houses around.

You could see anyone coming toward you
For at least a mile.
I asked the owner if this were a CIA house.
He laughed and said no.
I could see right through his denial.
He said he couldn't have one here
Because the neighbors were nosey.

Well, I told him we could either
Kill them all or hire them to watch for strangers.
I am going to call CIA headquarters
To apprise them of this ideal location.
I told the salmon house proprietor
To expect men in suits to soon appear.
He said, "I hope they like smoked salmon!"

I Miss Him

Every year I travel to the West Coast of Ireland
I live here for thirty days
Writing, walking, praying, absorbing
The surrounding expanse of bog and ocean.

By the end of three weeks
My heart starts to pain and
I realize I am missing Bryan Moser
He is thirty-six years old and we are always together.

He phones me every day
Today he reminded me
That we shall be together in four days
He was bubbling with joy.

When I leave him,
I always leave a part of my heart
At night when he is in bed
He calls my name out loud
As I do his.

No one could ever love me more than he.
My Indwelling God has bestowed him to me.
When I call his name out loud
I always remember that Bryan is God's son
I am just his dad on earth
I'll take that.

Does It Ever Become Old?

Fifteen years I have travelled to these shores
I never expected what would happen
To be accepted by one and all
To be loved by the Irish
To be loved by the animals
To be loved by the land.

Each day on Errislannan
As the ocean and shore crash together
As the flowers bend in the wind
I am baptized as a human once again
So sensitive to each minute change
Never ever the same.

Errislannan talks to her residents
The rocks guarding the bog speak
Of years past, of pain remembered
The roads tell their story
Of famine, of war, of love forgotten
And I am admitted into this chalice.
It is never the same
Never growing old
Never growing common
Never taken for granted
Always changing
Always Ireland.

Call Me Back Again

I shall soon be packing up my things
Leaving the shores of Errislannan
Gone for another year.
As I gaze out at your rocky shores
There is a worry inside me
That calls "Will you be here next year?"
Will your mist and rain
Ever again touch my face?
Will your mares and ponies
Gently eat from my hands?
Will your stone walls and bogs
Touch my feet and hands?
Oh, Errislannan, a love of my life,
Call me back again
I can hear your winds
Thousands of miles away
Call me back again
And I shall happily come
To rest in the bosom of your land
And once again share my life with you.

I Am a Fool

Off to Ireland
Passport
Money
Gore-Tex jacket
Climbing boots
On the plane to Shannon
I realize I have left my medications.

The most important item for my thirty day vacation
Is my medication.
So, I, the fool, decide to tell no one
I shall be Jack Armstrong, the all-American boy
I shall be the life of the party
And, I am,
For the first two days.

I have never had withdrawal symptoms from drugs
Because for the past fifteen years as a bi-polar man
I have never missed a day.
I had no idea what I would go through.
Chills, sweating profusely, shaking.
Finally I told the family members with me
I just didn't want to ruin their vacation.

I am a fool
Now everyone is in emergency mode.
After four days of "faking" feeling good I see a doctor
She looks at me and says
"We have pharmacies here
We have all your medications"
In five minutes, the proud fool
Becomes a humble fool.

Part II
Craziness

Spoons

Spoons is a game conceived by a goofy God.
There are spoons in the middle of a table.
Playing cards are passed secretly
When you get three of a kind
You quietly slip a spoon out
Hoping no one sees you.
When someone discovers a spoon missing
They wildly and deftly attempt to grab a spoon.
Since there are not enough spoons,
Someone ends the game sans spoon.
This game changes silent saints to rabid dogs.
People are screaming and grabbing
Threatening you with death
Holding a knife in a downward posture
Grabbing your arm with their teeth.
Not a game for the proud or dainty.

The Aircraft Bathroom

I am quite sure that sometime during your life
You have been on a commercial flight
And have had to use the toilet.
You quietly slip off your seat belt
You quickly head for the rest station
And "ugh."
You can hardly fit through the door.
You are in relatively good shape
You thought.
You turn sideways, pushing
For a moment you are stuck
Then "ugh," you are through.
Now comes the task of standing
Trying to accomplish what you came to do.
Not easy to turn
You use "baby steps" to move
Only to realize the plane is turning.
This is not a happy time!
I am going to contact the airlines
Recommending a toilet be attached
To each seat.
One would have a small curtain
That would surround you.
No squeezing
No baby steps
Just pure relief.

One of God's Gifts

I do believe that one of God's greatest gifts
Is *sleep*.
The final item that God made on the seventh day
Was the gift of rest.
Whenever I am manic
Whenever I am exhausted to the bone
Just frazzled and worn
My favorite companion, sleep,
Comes to my rescue.

I am convinced that God catches a wink
Every so often.
When he was daily walking the earth
Jesus would go off by himself
Presumably to pray.
How long do you think
He talked to his dad
Before his eyes would slowly close?
He was totally like us, save sin.

Well then, of course he took naps.
Praying and sleeping are an amazing combo.
Sleep carries us into our unconscious
Where we can hear more than the spoken word.
Makes sense to me.

Crayons

When I was a kid
You could buy ten crayons in a box.
There they were,
The only colors in the entire world.
Now, however, you can purchase a large box
Containing sixty-four colors.
This is mind-boggling to me!
Who ever heard of Mauve?
Or better still, you can color with Timberwolf.
I am extremely confused and upset,
My whole color world is in jeopardy.
I don't want to color with Jalapeño,
That is something I eat.
I shall never color with Scarlet
And that's final!

Parking Meters

When I was a kid
We had dozens of parking meters
Along Fifth Avenue in Brooklyn.
People would put money in them
If you parked your car in a certain space.

These meters were at least five feet tall.
As boys we competed in jumping over
These giant aluminum trees.
We started in a line,
Each of us would grab the top,
Jumping over without touching

For the boys who missed
The result was physically painful
And extremely humbling.
Everyone wanted to be Champion Jumper,
Not a shabby title for a ten-year-old
In the competitive world of New York.

This was the exciting life in a city
It was always about winning.
I am sure this and other feats
Made me who I am today.

The Whistler

The woman I love is a whistler
Notes float out of her mouth
That do not sound like any song
I have ever heard.

Can you imagine in her mind
The person in charge of music
Just hitting random notes
Standing next to the music machine?

Eyes closed
Pushing random keys
And blowing through her mouth
At the same time.

There must be a small chamber in her brain
Marked "who gives a rat's ass?"
This is where those strange sounding
Notes come from.

But, surprisingly she is happy
As a mockingbird
Just blowing notes that sound like "crap"
Happy as a pig in dirt.

Running Boards

Only the wise and elderly who read this
Will remember running boards on automobiles.
They were popular when I was a child.
Yesterday I witnessed a car with boards.

Those of us who grew up with them
Know they were placed beneath each door
You could then stand on them as the car moved.
When we were children we would get
Our scooters going down hill.

When we came alongside
We would reach out
Jumping onto the running board
Grabbing the door handle
The driver was never happy.

There were also boards
On the back of the electric trolleys
On Fifth Avenue in Brooklyn, New York.
You could ride free by jumping aboard
The wooden step on the rear.

Of course, this was illegal.
When you are ten years old
And a New Yorker
Nothing you do is illegal.
Nothing.

Cable Cars

In San Francisco
You must ride cable cars
The operator rings its bells
As we venture down a steep hill
"I'm coming, I'm coming," is his message
As he pulls and pushes strange metal gears.
Cable cars full of tourists.
Everyone taking pictures with smart phones
Leaning out into space, excited
It reminds me of the circus parade
Where cars full of animals would pass by.
We are all children at heart
So, climb aboard.

Smiling Jack

That is the name I was called in school
So, I have this theory about smiling
I believe that if I smile at an object
Which is alive
It then grows faster and happier.

I know you may judge me as strange
But the way I figure is that a smile
Certainly can't do anything bad
So there must be a positive glow
From my face to it.

I am aware of my eyes widening
As I smile
I know my heart pumps faster
My chest expands
My aura brightens.

I just love this idea.
Of course, every tree and plant
Smiling back at me
Has a chance of illuminating my life
It is a sure winner.
Thanks.

My Office Manager

My office manager is my son, Bryan Moser.
He takes his job very seriously.
If I speak out loud to myself
Saying that I need some item
He immediately goes on the Internet
Ordering at least two of the item.

He knows my credit card numbers
He uses them more than I do.
A new basketball shirt from Duke,
He's got it.
A football jacket from Notre Dame,
Of course.
My credit card bill is much like
A list of colleges in America.

My office is filled with important pieces
He orders plants
He keeps all the machines running
He purchases my professional cards
Listing appointment times and phone numbers
With the words "Go New York Rangers"
Prominently displayed on the front of each card.
My patients love this.

Sixteen Light Bulbs

Bryan Moser is my purchasing agent
At my office in Florida
He is extremely efficient at what he does
The problem is that he purchases
Enough items to last a lifetime.

Yesterday he procured sixteen light bulbs
I told him it would take me a lifetime
To use all these bulbs in our office
Since he is extremely sensitive
He did not take my comment lightly.

But this is not his only purchase
He has ordered enough envelopes
To last a hundred years
Yellow writing tablets are stacked high
Bank checks I could write forever
Pens and pencils are scattered everywhere.

I have decided to live only to 2100
I'll be 163 years old then
But I shall have used up
All his purchases
No big deal.
I can do this.

Bryan's Birthday

My special needs son, Bryan Moser,
Loves his birthday.
He is now thirty-six years old.
He starts planning his day
At least one month before the date.
He follows the same routine every year.
He gives me a written list
Of activities that he and I must do.
He writes them in large letters
On the back of an envelope.
Here is his list to me:
Plates
Forks
Cake knife
Pick up cookies and cream cake
Sing Happy Birthday to me
Open presents
Everyone leaves
Say goodbye.

Bryan Moser Calls Me

I have been at a psychology conference all day
I have not seen him or talked to him.
The phone rings, it is he
"Dad, I love you five hundred percent."
I never get over these love messages.
My heart just grows bigger.

All of a sudden
I don't have a worry in the world
No mental anguish
No physical pain
Bryan Moser loves me five hundred percent!

Does anyone know what that means to me?
Winning the lottery? No, better.
Being acclaimed the best therapist? No, better.
Him expressing his love for me. Yes. Yes.
A thousand times, yes!

Oak Trees

As I left my exercise class today
It was blustery and cold.
Standing in front of me
Was a young oak tree waving its arms.
Without thinking I said, "Good morning, oak."
Lo and behold, it said, "hello" back to me.
What a shock!

I told this oak that I had an oak, Fiona,
Who lived in front of my office, and we spoke.
"All the local oaks are familiar with Fiona
She has told us of your relationship."
I asked this new oak
If all oak trees talked to each other
"Of course," she said.

I never realized that this dialogue took place.
I was astonished that this tree
Located a mile from Fiona
Knew of our liaison.
There were all sorts of questions
In my mind.

Can trees talk to animals?
Are there many people who talk with trees?
Do oaks talk to pine and maple and spruce?
I can't wait until I come back here
And continue with my conversation.
I am so alive with all these possibilities!

Part III
The Human Factor

The Forgotten Ones

Yvonne Baratte was a resistance fighter
Who was arrested in Paris in 1944.
She died in Ravensbrück of dysentery.
She has long been forgotten
In the long journey of our world.

I shall not forget you, Yvonne Baratte.
I shall call your name out loud,
Each day for the rest of my life.
You are one of millions of forgotten
Amazing people who simply said "No"
To the Nazi invader.

I am in awe at the courage
You displayed in defying a predator nation.
You helped your French colleagues
Wrest Paris from the Germans.

No. I shall not forget you,
Yvonne Baratte!

My Small Friend

I live in a suburb.
Middle class families live all around me.
There is a local elementary school
Situated a few blocks from my home.
Every morning as I drive to work
I pass this little guy
Who is carrying a very large backpack.

Each day he looks at me and waves.
I do not know this boy,
I have never honked my horn at him
Nor said a word to him.
Yet each day he celebrates my journey.
I know this exchange is a
Spiritual gift.

If I am too early or too late
I do not see him.
I am at a point in my life
Where his greeting is a highlight
Of my day.
This phenomena has happened to me
At other times in my life.

If I attempt to discover where he lives
Then I never see him again
So I just am full of gratitude
Thanking God,
Since I know it is he.

The Emergency Room

My son Kevin is quite ill
I take him to a local emergency room
This place is a world unto itself
Fractures in wheelchairs
People with blood problems
Their skin grayish.
Young children in pain
Whimpering as they lie
On their mom's chest
Elderly people looking like
Auschwitz survivors
All exhausted, feeling vulnerable.

Time never moves in the E.R.
If anything it seems to go backward
When a name is called
Everyone else is wondering why
Their name has not been uttered.
Somehow, the large number of people
Starts to dwindle down
At four a.m. you hear your name
But by this time you really don't care
If anyone ever comes out
From the curtained area
And attends to you.

Behold Him

It was a dreary, dark night, as I drove home
I would not have seen him
If he had not raised his arm
I thought that this person might need help
I made a U-turn and drove back.

He was standing next to the airport parking lot
A small man with a scraggly beard
When I asked him if he was okay
He replied, "Yes."
I inquired if he needed money
He replied, "No."
"Well, can I help you in some way?" I said.

"Can you drive me home?" he asked.
"Of course I can," I replied
I opened the back door of my car
He didn't move at all.
His weak voice whispered
"I have Parkinson's Disease
My legs are weak."

He was shaking but it wasn't a cold night
When I looked at him
I thought I knew him
I sensed a holy presence
As I took hold of his arm
Easing him into my car.

He said he had been standing
For two hours but no one stopped
As I drove off he quietly said,
"Thank you."

When we arrived at his home
He could not get out of my car.

We struggled to get his legs out
As he continually said, "Thank you"
I told him how much I appreciated
His presence in my life
As I retrieved his baggage
He leaned against a stone wall
In his driveway.

There were fourteen steps up to his front door
He told me that he could make this
I repeatedly asked him if I could help
He looked at me and said,
"No, you have done what you needed to do."
It was then that I knew who he was.

As I drove off
I looked in my rearview mirror.
He stood with his hand upraised
I said out loud,
"Behold Him."

A Sense of Humor

My sense of humor saves me
I love to make up stories
Telling people all sorts of crazy things
I really do it more for me
Than for the audience at hand
I love to laugh at myself.

I can make up some beauties.
I think growing up in Brooklyn
With a dad who laughed a lot
Helps me when I am telling
A "whopper" of a story.
People aren't sure if what I am saying
Is true or not.

With all the heaviness I carry
In my heart for the world's poorest
I need to be lighthearted at times.
It keeps my spirit in balance.
If I didn't hold this humor
I'd be crying more.

But, remember
If you ever meet me face to face
Just realize that what I tell you
May just be plain "horse hockey."

Sofya Gulyak

She came on stage in a purple and black outfit
Not tall
Not short
Once she put her hands on the piano keys
Nothing but her music was evident.

Rachmaninoff's Third Piano Concerto
Runs more than forty minutes without break
She is the only woman pianist I know
Who can play this piece
I was spellbound.

I don't think I moved at all
I definitely did not breathe
I sat mesmerized
I knew I dwelled in "Music Heaven."

No one in the audience made a sound
No coughs. No sneezes
We were all caught up in this
Web of ecstasy.
These rare moments are sacraments
Given to us by a loving God.

The Men's Group

The five of us sat in a circle
Sharing our male experiences
All eager to discuss our pain
Knowing that this happening together
Rarely occurs in our lifetime.

Slowly out of our deepest being
Comes the sheer pain of male existence
All the misunderstanding
All the abandonment
If only we can get it all out.

Such good intentions we had
Such hopes for everlasting love
Such intense pain
Such tragic endings.

We were like five teenagers
Discussing puppy love with hope
Oh, how we had looked everywhere
Oh, how we dreamt of love
Only to be left without a trace.

God, where has she gone?
In the frenetic pace of life
Have we somehow missed her?
God would you just bring her back,
If only for a moment.

She Is My Sister

I flew to New York
To visit my sister, Joan.
She is eighty and suffers from dementia.
Surprisingly she was in high spirits.
She was remembering past experiences
Which I had totally forgotten.

Her tiny body lies under covers.
She seemed happy as we discussed
The good old days.
I thought that there are still
Good brain cells in her.

We looked at pictures
Which were taken seventy years ago.
She told me when and where they happened.
She was correct.
I didn't remember any of it
So, who has dementia?

Tomorrow my sister won't remember a thing
But today is Joan's day.
She is the Moser Family Historian
Waxing eloquent on the old times
Totally in control of her universe.

The Twirling Young Girl

She was standing in front of me
As Bryan and I waited at Dunkin Donuts.
I would guess that she was ten years old
Standing next to her mom.

Her pink and purple skirt was perfect
Her sneakers lined with pink
Quietly leaning against her mom
Knowing that mom would always support her.

All of a sudden
Without any fanfare
She started to twirl
She was the prima ballerina
In Dunkin Donuts' Swan Lake

What an unexpected gift
A dancing beauty in the early morning
Everyone watched her
Totally mesmerized
By her beauty

Thank you, Shekhinah
For this unforgettable picture
A ballerina in a coffee shop
We were truly blessed.

My Cousin, Jack

My cousin died on May 2, 2000
He was my closest friend
We didn't agree on many issues
But we deeply loved each other
There was such goodness inside him
That wherever he went
A bright light followed.

I often think of him
At age six, we were wrestling
At age fourteen, we were still wrestling
He was the perfect Catholic
I was the constant heretic
He was always giving me advice
Which I never followed.

I do miss him
I am fortunate to have other men
Who have taken his place
Yet no one do I love more than he
He constantly sends me messages
Giving me his heavenly advice
I continue to turn off my headset
Hearing nothing
Our relationship now is just right.

The Drummer

I have always walked to a different drummer.
I can hear its beat every day
Over the years the sound has changed
From a loud drum to a quiet harp.
I no longer run into the street
When I hear my favorite sound
The drummer and I have agreed
To focus on music just for peace and justice
I still walk with passion
But my angry notes have disappeared
The drummer and I have never been happier.

I Love You, Grandpa

There is nothing sweeter to hear,
Nothing sweeter in the universe.
When we are together my granddaughters
Just love on me.
I am easily the richest man
Initially, they come up to me
Placing their arms around me
Looking up with blue eyes
They utter the magic words
Oh, so softly.
And all is well with
Grandpa.

The Brown Bag

She carries this dilapidated brown thing
Everywhere she goes.
Weddings, funerals, work, vacation
It is there over her shoulder.
She looks much like Gunga Din
On a busy day, carrying water to the thirsty.

What you don't understand
Is that this bag is her.
She carries her dreams and hopes
Her joy and sorrows
Her intimate thoughts
All placed gently within.

Gifts for others.
Her bubbling personality
Her pain and grief
It is all there
In the brown, wrinkled thing
As her life goes on.

My Japanese Fishing Village

When I was in Vietnam
I ripped up my knee.
I was medivaced to the
Naval Hospital in Yokosuka.
After the surgery
I was encouraged to walk,
Ride bikes for a thorough recovery.

Each day I left the naval base
Riding my bike to the top of a knoll
Where I could see the Sea of Japan.
Below me was a small Japanese village
They were fisherman
Normally unloading their catch
When I arrived.

I would sit atop the hill
Writing and praying.
After a few weeks of this
When I got off my bike
There would be a small dish
Filled with pieces of fish
From my village below.

This beautiful practice continued
Until I departed, returning to Vietnam
That was in April of 1967.

In September of 1973
I was returning home to the USA
I had been stationed in Manila.
My family was with me,
My wife and six children.
We stopped in Tokyo.
I took them all by train to Yokosuka.

We all walked to the grassy knoll
Where six years before I had dwelled.
As soon as I looked down
To view my Japanese fishing village
My Japanese friends saw me.
All of them peered up at us.

Then all of a sudden
They pointed their fingers at me
And all bowed.
I'll never forget it
We all bowed in return.
I never felt more loved.

She Lived in a Haze of Waiting

She lived in a haze of waiting
Not sure if he would come.
As she peered out her window
She pulled the curtain back
To be sure she could see him coming.
She had only been with Martin
A dozen times during the past year
But there was an instant togetherness.
She would leave tomorrow for Dublin
Where she would start university.
The rain poured down on this cold night.
She prayed he would come
To see her one last time.

Early in the dark of night
She heard a pebble hit her window.
She was fully clothed lying on her bed
She jumped to the window
He was soaked to the skin
With a wet blanket wrapped around.
Without saying a word
They kissed.
He held her in his arms
For what seemed like days.
As the sun rose
He was gone

When she returned home
Following her first semester,
Her mother told her that
Martin had died of consumption.
She felt weak in the knees
Grabbing a kitchen chair for support
She closed her eyes remembering him
Crossing the bog in a rainstorm.
He loved her.
She had experienced wonderful dreams
Of them being together for life.

She thought that it would be
A very long time, if ever,
Before she felt for another
What she felt for him.
She would once again start
Passing through the haze
Of waiting
Except now she knew
What love was like
Remembering Martin
Realizing that she had been loved.

The Great Wind

The Native American believes that
He is being carried across the sky
By the Great Wind.
He need not worry or complain
The wind always takes him
To where he needs to be.
Such is the make-up of faith.

Why does it seem so difficult
For the rest of us to gain the faith?
All is well.
The great God of Wind handles life
I just need to hang on
Enjoy the ride
And be *aware*.

Part IV

Darkness

Darkness

Beware of darkness
It slips inside so easily
The hopelessness around you
Will break your heart
In a heavy unforgiving way.

The immense pain of life is everywhere
And we can't perform miracles
Easing the pain
Turning to prayer may help
But God works extremely slowly.

It is as if this God puts pain aside
Getting back to it when there is time
So there is some acceptance necessary
On our part.

If you attempt to understand the darkness
You are bound to discover nothing
Darkness exists for whatever reason
Unbeknownst to our feeble mind.

Embrace those who are in pain
Karma works
Easing their pain, eases ours
Yet darkness will always persist
Regardless of what we do.

Coming Together

Parents of a suicide son
Grieving beyond belief
Never saw it coming
He didn't let anyone know
His final phone call to his brother:
"I have fought this feeling
All my life. I can't do this anymore.
I know what I am doing."

Early one June morning
He walked into the Gulf of Mexico
Gone without a trace
We sat close together
Holding hands
Parents hoping to discover why
But knowing that they never will.

The grief was so thick
It was difficult to breathe.
"Oh, my son, if only I knew
Of your pain."

All they can do now
Is to celebrate his spirit
Listening to his friends
As they praise his efforts
To love all those around him
Maybe his story will save
Another from this despair.

"Oh, my son, if only I knew
Of your pain."

If God Mourns

If God mourns the death of its son
Who mourns our death and darkness?
Maybe Yahweh does take time to
Grieve on our behalf
If that be true
There must be no time for anything else
Mourning the billions
Constantly calling names out loud
There is something wrong
With this sad picture
The God I love is all
Forgiveness, kindness, and love
When does God have time for this?
I am at a loss,
Always will be.

The Children of Stones

They live with daily brutality
They are taught at an early age
To kill Israelis.
In the name of Allah
They attempt to perform this work.

The hatred in their hearts is palpable
Their only weapon is stones
Young men throwing stones
At an army which possesses
All modern sophisticated weaponry.

These teenagers know that these rocks
May not kill.
They just don't know what else to do.
They call out loud the names of dead relatives
And the name of Allah
As they hurl stones.

The children of stones
Have lived with injustice
All their lives.
It is David and Goliath again.
They will eventually prevail.

I Could Have Saved Two More

When Schindler says this out loud
My heart breaks.
Haven't we all uttered the same words?
I could have done more
Isn't it a pity?
We hold back for some reason
We have done enough
And that's it.
Don't ask me to do any more.

But, there are always two more.
There are always those we can't see.
Reach out again
Reach into the darkest corner
They are there
Don't stop now
They are so close
Two more.
Just two more.

The Deep Pit

There are times when I slip into the pit
I don't see this coming
There doesn't seem to be an apparent cause
It just happens out of the blue.

I can do nothing
I register zero on my energy scale
I pray to Shekhinah
But I remain locked in no man's land
Until she decides to bring me back.

When I am dwelling in the pit
I think of everything negative
I am a bad person
I have Alzheimer's
I am a poor parent.

When I finally do emerge
Popping up to the surface
I am grateful and reassured
Thinking I have learned,
Only to fall again into the pit
Months later.

Power Concedes Nothing

Do you believe the powerful of the world
Are interested in a carbon-free atmosphere?
Do you think the wealthiest of the world
Worry about the use of fossil fuels?
Do you think that losing 22,000 children every day
From the disease of malaria
Keeps them up at night?
Of course not.
The financial profits in energy are enormous.
Certainly, too big to be stopped.

Love your neighbor?
I don't think so.
Be your brother's keeper?
Not in your lifetime.
Greed is the bottom line.
We are the land of the rich
And the home of the poor.

Power concedes nothing.
It just claims everything
Leaving the rest of the world bereft.
So you believe that capitalism
Is our best choice?

The Poor Are Blessed

Really?
The poor are blessed, you say.
Really.
That is what the rich say
Maybe I'll just ask a poor person
If she feels so blessed.

Each day for the poor is a challenge
Find food
Find medicine
Find health
Find jobs
Find money
Find security
Find God

Their children die of illnesses
Which are curable.
Their daughters are raped.
Their sons die in war.
Their husbands vanish.
Are you sure they are blessed?

It is not that I think you are lying
It just seems that life declares
That the poor are not blessed.
Can you see where I am coming from?

Even The Lost

Even the lost are redeemed.
Maybe this is the way it all works.
All the dead must come back to life
Finally celebrating their entire existence.
People who were separated reappear together.
All the pain experienced
Is transformed into truth and beauty.
The earthly lost are heavenly saved.
Jubilation.
Everyone makes it.

Survivors of Stalin's Gulag

They finally left the gulag
With nothing but fear.
They trusted no one.
They were even terrified
By their own thoughts.
They discussed their life in the camp
With no one,
Not even family.

Their life has been completely taken.
No friends,
Never leaving their home,
Believing in nothing,
They were totally dead to life,
Slowly disintegrating
Into nothingness.

They called the camp their Golgotha.
They had been emotionally crucified
Even though they were given their bodies back
They knew they had no life.
Death was their only ally.

Even God didn't recognize them.
They lived in a dark, dreary place
Called Anonymity.
All twenty million of them.

PTSD

He can't make eye contact with me
He is ashamed of who he is
And what he has done
After four tours in a foreign land
He is full of doubt and anger
But can't as yet open his heart.

I tell him that we shall take his journey together
He has heard this before from other therapists
He just sits staring into the distance
As he opens his mouth to speak
Tears slowly slide down his cheeks.

"I was ready to kill myself last night
But I got so drunk I passed out," he says.
We talk about being here for one another
He knows I had fought in Vietnam
I give him my cell phone number.

He talks a few minutes about his time
In the Korengal Valley in Afghanistan.
He moves closer, sitting on the end of his chair
We are brothers of combat
As he rises from his chair he says,
"I'll come back tomorrow."
But, he doesn't.

Railroad Cars

In the city I live in
We have numerous train tracks
Cutting across many of our busiest streets.
Every time I am held up at a train crossing
I start looking for the wooden cars
Where you can see through
The space between beams.
When one of these cars crosses my gaze
I look closely to see if there are
People inside pressed together like sardines
I know they are heading to death camps.

You would think that by now
I would be free of the Holocaust ghosts.
Alas, I am not
Nor, shall I ever be.
In many ways,
Those railroad cars still run
Through many countries
Carrying the poor and unfortunate
Where they pay the price
For the world's greed and selfishness.

Why Are We Always So Surprised?

We are the largest war machine
In the history of this world.
We have military men in over one hundred countries.
Our war budget is bigger than the next ten adversaries.
Our money for offense takes from our poor,
Our education, medicine and disease prevention.

We have drones that kill both civilian and military
We have plutonium laced bullets
Which spread nuclear death.
We assassinate.
We start wars for no reason.
We torture prisoners.

Why are we always so surprised
When other people want to kill us?
They behead us.
They torture us.
They terrorize our country.
Why are we always so surprised?

The Scandals

The year 2014 has been fraught with disasters.
Wars
Ebola
Millions of refugees
Environmental mishaps.

To me the most hideous
And the least mentioned of all these
Is the genocide in Palestine and Gaza
Do I pray to Shekhinah
Reading the Kabbalah?
Yes, I do.

Do I blame the Israelis for this catastrophe?
Absolutely, yes.
The world says very little about this
Since they fear retribution from Israel.
What cowards free men have become!
The prophets from the Old Testament
Are crying in outrage over this.

Why can't just one head of state
Tell the world the truth?
Can we not take blinders off
And see what is happening?
It is the saddest of human conditions
If any nation should notice this,
It is Israel.
Shame on you.

The Falling Place

There are times in my life
When I am at the falling place
I am tipping backwards
With no one behind me
To break my fall.

I have no earthly reason to be in depression
Without noticing a small piece of black matter
Quietly slips inside my brain
Settling in for an indefinite stay
There is no light whatsoever.

Only Shekhinah has the gift
Of carrying a beam of light
Into the abyss.
I know I can pick out the light
At the end of a long tunnel
I see myself walking toward it
But I don't seem to be closing
The distance.

Part V

The End Is Not Our Enemy

The End Is Not Our Enemy

Believe me, death is nothing to fear
I have already experienced this
The end is something I dream about
To finally be together with the Indwelling God
It is much like New Year's Eve
In New York City
Except that the New Year's ball
Goes up, not down
The Celestial Orchestra is
Made up of all deceased family members
The Chorus consists of old buddies
From the streets of Brooklyn.

The end of this life
Believe me, is not our enemy
It is rather an awesome beginning
A lightness of being
A constant sunrise
Please believe me in this.

Jack, Be Still

It is extremely difficult for me to be still
Even though God tells me that It can handle life
I still believe that I must do something
To help bring about God's desire.

Time and again the message to me is,
Jack, be still
Still I think that God needs my help
What is so wrong with me?

One drawback is that I am a male
I believe I can do a better job
than God can.
What arrogance!

Secondly, I desire to stay in control
I'll fix the world when I am good and ready,
"thank you very much."
It is truly laughable.

God must get tired
Dealing with me.

Judas Iscariot

For centuries Judas has been vilified.
Now with the discovery of the Gospel of Judas
Theologians have commenced to revise his story.
The Gospel depicts Judas as the only disciple
Who understood what Jesus was doing.
Judas is the one who leads the way
Jesus revealed to Judas what he must do
Judas then performed for him
The greatest service so necessary
He turned over his Lord
So that Jesus could finally
Escape the confines of his body.
For his best friend,
Judas had to do what he did.
No doubt Judas is the greatest
Of all the disciples
But, we know that the
Official Christian churches will
Change nothing.
How sad is that?

Mary Magdalene

They called her a prostitute
But she was not.
She was one of Jesus's most trusted disciples.
The Gospel of Mary Magdalene
Shows her closeness to Jesus
Physical touch, yes.
His wife, yes.
He was exactly like us
Without sin
She was woman.
He man.

Interbeing

We are all one.
When we turn and look back
We realize we all started from two beings
Who evolved from gas, water, rock, and sun.
When we love another
We love ourselves
When we kill another
We kill ourselves.
We all hang on the vast web of life.
When one person moves
We all move.
Like it or not
We are all one.
Your mother indeed
Is my mother.

Layaway Prayers

We perform the "layaway thing" before Christmas
We then pay an amount each month
Until we have finally paid off our debt.
It is the identical way with our prayers.

I have been praying for justice many years
A few days ago a thought came to me
That God was going to use all my prayers
To bring about justice in one instance
Of injustice in the world.

The idea just popped into my head.
I knew it was a hint from Shekhinah.
It made such sense to me,
Of course, God had saved my prayers.
Of course, God would use them when ready.

This revelation brought great joy to my heart.
Somewhere in the world at that moment
My prayers were being used
Every syllable of uttered prayer.
Jubilation!

The Crack in Everything

Imperfection is the key
Mistakes are wonderful and necessary.
There is no perfect anything.
Why then do we attempt to be perfect?
Light always slips through the crack.
It is the only brightness
We'll ever need.
From here we can see who we are.
We can happily live the imperfect life.

Where Am I?

Nearer to Shekhinah?
Closer to ego?
Listening to Jesus?
Desiring and clinging?
Just because I learn more
As I grow older,
Doesn't necessarily mean
That I am any wiser.
It is good for me to get away
From my life in Florida
Where I think I am special.
Coming to Ireland
Where I am no one
Is extremely good for my humility.
"Keep me invisible, Lord,"
I do not need any *attention*
Yet, the need to be noticed
Slips silently into my brain.
"Get away from me,"
It is Satan at his best.
Please help me at last to find my cave
So that I can hibernate
And become less.

Bi-Polar

It is a curse I live with every day.
I have no idea when either beast, depression or mania,
Will occupy my mind.

It always takes me by surprise.
It sneaks around the corner of my brain and
Boom, it hits me.
Never see it coming.
I can deal with mania better
My personality is normally slightly manic.
I have a gift of gab
And I am the life of the party.

Depression is certainly my unseen enemy.
I have nothing to be depressed about.
I am loved.
I am surrounded by friends.

Depression never knows when to leave
And I can't press the correct buttons
Which cause it to vanish.
It humbles me.
I try to make excuses to those around me.
I put the "Gone Fishing" sign on my door
And just wait for it to pass.

He Was Like Us in All Things

The bible is very explicit
Regarding Jesus's humanity.
Why then is it so difficult
To believe that Jesus and Mary Magdalene
Loved each other?

Common sense would tell us
That this occurrence could easily
Have transpired.
Why do we believe that celibacy
Is more holy than loving
Another in sexual ways?

Just because Christian churches
Tell us one thing
Doesn't mean that this is right.
The churches in 2014
Have not discussed any of
The following topics:

Brothers and sisters of Jesus
The Gospel of Judas
The Gospel of Mary Magdalene
The possibility that Judas
Was the greatest disciple
The possibility that Mary Magdalene
Was Jesus's closest disciple.

Use your imagination,
Which is much more a gift
Than knowledge or brilliance.
I can easily see Jesus, the man,
Loving Mary, the woman.
It is a union made by the Father.

Amen.

My Singing Sweetheart

The female in my life loves to sing.
Believe me, I love her dearly
But she has no voice. None.
When she sings our National Anthem
They take the flag down!

Amazingly, the one group
Who absolutely loves her voice
Is cows.
Daily she walks the narrow trails
Of Western Ireland, singing.

Every cow within range
Comes over to the stone walls
Along the road, tail wagging
Head swaying to the beat of her notes.
Just a musical miracle to behold.

As she passes the cows
They all walk to the end of their pasture.
At this point, they all start mooing
In a sort of harmony.
It is the worst dissonance I have ever heard.

I'll bet if that farmer
Checked the output of milk
From these mooing cows
He would discover that they produce
Much more milk than his other animals.
"Fair play to you, my love."

My Judith

She is lost when I am in depression
She looks for a lever to pull
Or a button to push.
There must be something she can do, she thinks,
But, alas, only patiently waiting is the remedy.
Of course, I am trying everything
To pull away from the depression gravity
Which is not possible
But, I try anyway.
It is like getting gum on your shoe.
No matter how many times
You pull your foot up
Scraping it on the gravel
It just never all leaves.

So, my love,
All you can do is swallow
Paint on your easel
Listen to your music
Walk the roads alone
And wait.
I shall come to you
When I can
Loving you into wonder
Forgetting my departure
Celebrating my return.